Copyright Page:

Cleanse My Home © Copyright 2022 Tracey Waite

All rights reserved. No part of this publication may be reproduced, distributed, or transmitted in any form or by any means, including photocopying, recording, or other electronic or mechanical methods, without the prior written permission of the publisher, except in the case of brief quotations embodied in critical reviews and certain other non-commercial uses permitted by copyright law.

Although the author and publisher have made every effort to ensure that the information in this book was correct at press time, the author and publisher do not assume and hereby disclaim any liability to any party for any loss, damage, or disruption caused by errors or omissions, whether such errors or omissions result from negligence, accident, or any other cause.

Neither the author nor the publisher assumes any responsibility or liability whatsoever on behalf of the consumer or reader of this material. Any perceived slight of any individual or organization is purely unintentional.

Cleanse my Home

The resources in this book are provided for informational purposes. Neither the author nor the publisher can be held responsible for the use of the information provided within this book.

For more information, email:

cleansemyhouse@gmail.com

Dedication

To my husband, Kevin, who has always believed I can put my mind to anything. He is the only person who has ever truly understood me and has been in sync with my beliefs and spirituality from the very beginning. He truly is my best friend and soulmate.

To my children, Edward, Grace and Olivia who have brought more joy into my life than I ever thought possible. You make me laugh, you make me cry, you make me shout and you make me proud. You are my biggest achievement in life.

To my step-children, Vicky, Steph, Hannah and Moya. Thank you for accepting me into your family and lives. I didn't grow up thinking I was going to be a step-mother but it is one of the favourite things about my life.

To my mum, who has stood by me through thick and thin. She is always there when I need her the most.

And finally, my inspiration, mentor and tutor …. Caroline. You were always my inspiration and guide when I needed it and always guiding me in the right direction. I don't know where you are now, but I hope that you and your family are happy and healthy.

TABLE OF CONTENTS

Introduction .... page 7

Chapter 1:
    Predecessor Law .... page 14

Chapter 2:
    Protection .... page 17

Chapter 3:
    What do I need? .... page 22

Chapter 4:
    Clutter .... page 28

Chapter 5:
    Preparations .... page 32

Chapter 6:
    'The Cleansing' .... page 37

Chapter 7:
    Australian Bush Flower Essences ...... page 45

Chapter 8:
Feng Shui ....page 51

Chapter 9:
The Bagua ....page 56

Chapter 10:
Geopathic Stress ....page 69

Chapter 11:
Bonus Chapter
'The Wish Bomb'................................page 76

Summary ....page 79

Bibliography..page 81

Wish list/notes ....page 82

Introduction:

Who Am I?

My name is Tracey Waite and back in 1998 I spotted the launch issue of Feng Shui for Modern Living in my local shop. I thought "that looks interesting", bought it and was hooked from then on. After a few months, I felt like I needed more information and attended my first Feng Shui course in February 1999, which was run by a lovely lady called Caroline. I went on to do lots of courses including learning about Geopathic stress and Space clearing.

As well as being a mother to three, stepmother to four, nana to nearly six (one on the way) and wife to a very understanding husband, I have a number of successful businesses in the beauty and wedding sectors – all which have had the benefit of space clearing. What started off as an interesting hobby has become a passion and lifestyle.

I love, love, love cleansing spaces, it feels so amazing - particularly good for clearing previous energy or if there has been illness/divorce. I always mini cleanse if we go away and stay in a hotel room (as there is lots of other people's energy) or in a new work space. It is also great for businesses, especially if you are taking over a space where the previous business has failed.

I moved into my most recent home 12 years ago and I knew as soon as I stepped inside it was the right home for me and my family, even though the house was a wreck, no gas, electricity or even water. There was no kitchen or bathroom even though the owner was still living in the house! The previous owner had ripped everything out in a bid to scupper the house sale. The owners has split acrimoniously, and the husband was doing his best to stop the house from selling as he didn't want to give his estranged wife any money.

However, I fell in love with the house!! But there was no way we could live in here with the old energy from the previous owners (this is called Predecessor Law, covered in the first chapter) so before we moved in I cleansed the whole house and cleared all the geopathic stress (covered in chapter 8).

We have now been in the house nearly 13 years and I love my home more than ever (even though there is slightly more clutter than I need). Writing this book has been cathartic and a reminder of what I should also be doing in my own home.

In the book I have also covered the basics of feng shui, how to use a bagua map, geopathic stress and clearing clutter as these are also important for having a happy and healthy home. However, out of everything I would say clearing negative energy is the first thing you should always do, followed by checking for geopathic stress. You can then start to work on the clearing any clutter and feng shui of your house.

*****

Space Clearing/Cleansing Your Home

I will use the term 'space clearing' a lot in this book, which is what I was taught when training. The term just means clearing negative energy from any space.

Space clearing is a very efficient method for renewing and cleansing the energy in structures, including homes, workplaces, schools, hospitals, and even your car.

The walls, floors and furniture of a structure will energetically record every movement and feeling that takes place there. Strong feelings, recurring physical or emotional patterns, both good and bad, can leave a lasting impression on a building's structure. How many of us have entered a room where an argument had just ended and remarked to a friend that "you could have cut the air with a knife," referring to how thick the tension was?

Our homes serve as reflections of who we are, as well as our aspirations. For instance, if someone is struggling in a relationship, it is almost guaranteed that the energy in that area of their home is blocked—either literally by clutter or energetically by stagnant energy.

Cleanse my Home

Our homes' energy is purified and revitalised through space clearing, which improves the quality of our lives. Space clearing is particularly effective when used in conjunction with geomancy (the art of detecting and clearing geopathic stress) and also manifesting – as you are putting all your future goals and aspirations into your home.

*****

Cleanse my Home

Smudging – what is it?

The word "smudging" is an English term derived from the word smudge. It refers to the act of burning sage, which is an ancient spiritual ritual widely used by the Indigenous peoples, in which sacred herbs and medicines are burned as part of a ritual or for cleansing or healing purposes.

Smudging is the practice of burning dried sage and the smoke is then wafted to remove negative energy (cleansing and purifying the space or person).

The herbs used for smudging produce smoke, which is deeply symbolic; the smoke is said to attach itself to the negative energy being banished as it ascends to heaven as if bringing any prayers and intentions up to the gods.

*****

Covid-19

Over the last few years, the covid-19 pandemic as completely changed the way we work. With more people than ever working from home, spaces that we once reserved for eating, sleeping and relaxing now have to serve an entirely new purpose.

Having to spend more time inside due to lockdowns and quarantines has no doubt made our physical spaces matter more. Quarantine has highlighted the impact that our homes can have on both our physical and mental health, so it is vitally important that our homes are a positive, healthy and revitalising place to both live and work.

Chapter 1

Predecessor Law

The Predecessor Law states that history repeats itself. Generally, what occurs in a space occurs again. We have all heard of homes that seem to have bad luck (due to divorce or marital problems, health issues, family problems). We all know of houses where the owners always seem to end getting divorced!

Take a look the homes in the area that you currently live. Can you think of any homes that seem to sell time and time again, any homes that appear to be run down and uncared for, any homes where everyone who moves in seems to have terrible luck in some way, or any homes that have been on the market for a long time?

Take my own story of buying my current house. Had I not cleansed my home, I probably would have ended up in the same situation as the previous owners – divorced and possible estranged from my children!

The same issues that affect homes can also affect businesses. Due to financial difficulties, an established company has to stop trading. The company is subsequently sold (or gone bust) and then new owners take over the location or building. They then also fail, and the situation will keep repeating again and again until the energy has been cleared.

My hometown of York is a perfect example. Unfortunately, there are so many shops and store fronts that have repeatedly closed down under different owners and businesses, but all have failed. Unfortunately, I can't clear a whole city, however much I would love to try.

*****

What can be done?

We will always find ourselves drawn to particular homes for reasons we may not completely understand – sometimes we just 'know' and you should always purchase a home if it feels good to you. Should you purchase a house in the future that had a negative previous owner, if you follow the instructions on space clearing and remove any negative energy you should stop the same thing from happening again.

Cleansing your home can raise the energy within your home and can clear the unseen energies within the space. Cleansing a home involves clearing what you cannot see or touch and is totally invisible. It can lift you and raise your own energy. After cleansing your home, you will feel that there is more of a purpose in life and that your personal goals can be attained. It is an excellent way of clearing out and starting afresh. If you feel stuck in your life then a space clear can give you clarity of thought. Always ensure that reason why you are carrying out a space clear is clear in your mind as you fill the space with your thoughts, your aspirations and goals.

Chapter 2

Protection

Why the need to protect yourself?

In my family, we call it 'bubbling'. We are grounding and protecting ourselves in certain situations and life in general. We always 'bubble' when travelling, particularly by aeroplane.

When you are working with energies it is important that you 'protect' yourself. This can take seconds and will help us in so many ways. For example, a reflexologist will protect themselves prior to treating a patient to ensure that they themselves do not pick up any negativity from the patient. We tend to take on board other people's problems more than we realise. You may have a friend who after being in their presence for some time makes you feel drained. Protection will help you to stop absorbing those negative energies around you.

Grounding Exercise

This is a simple easy to follow exercise that can be done in seconds. Sit in a relaxed position and be aware of your breathing. Imagine your body and where you are. Focus your mind on the earth beneath you and get a sense of your connection with it. If you are several floors up, imagine the connection going down through all the floors below you. Feel this connection going deeper into the earth. Sense this connection with the earth down through the soles of your feet and down through the base of your spine. Sense the energy going from the base of the spine right down to the centre of the earth and then looping back up to the spine - you are now grounded. This exercise will need to be repeated on a regular basis to feel the full effect.

*****

Protection Exercise (or 'bubbling')

Get comfortable and relaxed. Breathe gently in a relaxed rhythm. Imagine a beam of white light entering the top of your head. The white light permeates your head, chest, arms, torso, down into your legs and into your body so that your whole body is covered in a bright white light. Now imagine that this white light grows outside your body and spins in a clockwise direction and that you are now surrounded by a transparent protective bubble which protects you from any negative vibrations.

Sense this bubble all around your body, extending under your feet and above your head. Imagine that your own vibrations can exit the bubble and that good energy can enter the bubble. Have a clear sense that any external and unwanted negative energies cannot penetrate your bubble.

If you pick up of any negative feelings or illnesses from others, cover yourself in violet light.

This is my go-to for protection as it is quick and easy. My children all have their own ways of bubbling which includes lots of emoji's attached to their bubbles. Whatever works for you is fine.

An example of my bubbling …. When we travel on an aeroplane, I will bubble myself, my husband and each of my children. I will then put us all in one big family bubble and finish with a big bubble around the aeroplane – triple protection! Sometimes the bubble is gold, sometimes its blue, sometimes it is pink – there is no right or wrong way to do this, it is whatever feels right. I then visualise take off, landing and arriving safely.

I also do the same on a long car journey, I will bubble myself, any occupants and the car. I also visualise the journey and arriving safely at my destination.

Any situation where you feel nervous or anxious, just bubble. It helps you feel more confident and able to cope. For maximum benefit do the bubbling exercise daily for a few weeks.

If visualising is not your thing, I recommend you use is the 'golden ray of Christ' method. All you need to do is say the following three times:

'I now invoke the gold ray of Christ for my total protection, it is done.'

I sometimes use this as an extra layer of protection when cleansing homes.

"Always put protection in place when dealing with energy"

Chapter 3

What do I need?

Fresh flowers
A small arrangement either in a vase or an arrangement of flower heads on a saucer with a little water with a tealight in the middle. I have special saucers that were passed to me by my grandma, which I only use for space clearing.

Incense
The best incense to use for cleansing your home is **Nitiraj Incense Original** *which is great for helping shift negative energy.*

Incense holders

Bell
I use a Tibetan hand bell, which were originally used throughout the Himalayan regions of Nepal, Tibet and India. They are inexpensive and you can pick them up on Amazon for as little as £5. However, any bell will suffice, it's about

purifying and harmonising your space with sound.

Harmony balls
I have 2 sets of harmony balls. A set that the client uses to put their intentions and aspirations into, and another set I use which is neutral and infused with peace, love and harmony. You only require one set when doing your own cleanse and these, again, can be picked up on Amazon (you don't need to go any specialist sites).

Crystal
I personally like to use smoky quartz as it helps with dissolving negative energy, feelings and emotions, but any crystal you are drawn to is fine.

Sea Salt
Cleanses and heals.

Bush Flower Essences
These are used to make your own cleansing spray, however, you can buy your own ready-made spray easily (the one from Australian Bush Flowers does the job nicely). For more information, please refer to chapter 5.

Spring Water
Needed if you are making your own spray.

Atomiser
Needed if you are making your own spray.

Tealights

American white sage
For smudging. You will also need a fireproof bowl for catching the ash.

Matches

*****

Examples of what you need:

Flower arrangement	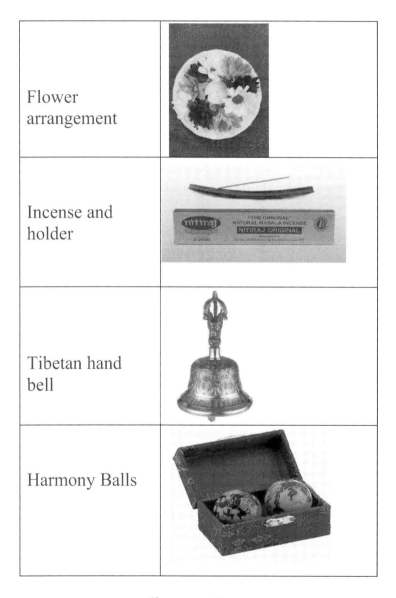
Incense and holder	
Tibetan hand bell	
Harmony Balls	

Cleanse my Home

Smokey quartz	
Australian bush flower spray	
White sage sticks	

Cleanse my Home

An example of a table setting

*****

Cleanse my Home

Chapter 4

Clutter

Clear your Clutter

The Oxford dictionary defines clutter as 'a crowded and untidy collection of things'.

Part of your preparations should be to try and de-clutter, however, do not put off cleansing your home if this seems a daunting task. If you are moving into a new home however, the perfect time to do a space clear is before you move your things in. Sometimes this isn't possible so as soon as possible after you have moved in is fine.

Categories of clutter:
- Things you do not use or love
- Things which are untidy or disorganized
- Too many things in too small a space
- Anything unfinished

The Clutter test:
- Does it lift my energy when I think about it or look at it?
- Do I absolutely love it?
- Is it genuinely useful?

If the answer is not a resounding 'yes' to all those questions, then what is it doing in your life?

Clutter zones:
- Drawers – particularly bedroom and kitchen
- Kitchen cupboards
- Tops of wardrobes
- Under beds
- Under the stairs
- Behind doors
- Dresser tops
- Loft space (represents your higher aspirations and your future)
- Cellar (represents your subconscious and your past)
- Garage, shed, garden
- Handbags

Now, I'm all for decluttering and before I had my children, I was absolutely brutal with what I kept and what I didn't. However, it is very easy to get into the habit of keeping things just in case and I, more than anybody, know that I shouldn't keep things that don't bring joy. This goes for kids' toys and all the other junk they and teens tend to keep hold off (don't get me started on my teenage girls rooms!).

Sorting out your life by sorting out your junk results in a tremendous renewal of your life force energy. It is something practical and tangible you can do actively to help yourself. If you know you are prone to hoarding, make a new rule for yourself - when something new comes in, something old goes out - at least your clutter will be changing even if it's not decreasing yet!

When your available space is filled with clutter, there is no room for anything new to come into your life. Your thoughts tend to dwell in the past, and you feel bogged down with problems which have dogged you for some time. You tend to look back rather than forward in your life, blaming the past for your current situation rather than taking responsibility for creating a better future. Clearing your clutter allows you to begin to deal with your problems and move forward. You have to release the past to create a better tomorrow.

"Keeping things 'just in case' indicates a lack of trust in the future"

Chapter 5

Preparations

Once you have all your supplies and you've hopefully managed to clear some clutter, you are now ready to start your preparations:

Clear any clutter - Very important, sometimes that's all you need to do (see chapter 3)

Physically clean the space - Cobwebs, dust, stagnant energy

Shower – also drink plenty of water to purify yourself

Put protection in place - See chapter 2. Use whichever protection suits you best

Remove any metal jewellery - Metals stops the flow of energy

<u>Make sure you are well and not nervous or fearful</u> - (avoid during menstruation)

<u>Work alone, or with someone who knows what is happening</u>

<u>Work in silence</u> - If someone else is with you, explain no talking and turn off your mobile, unplug your landline.

<u>Open windows and put away food</u> - Sage and incense can taint food

<u>Prepare your table and flowers</u>

Set your table - As near to your front door as you can, set a pretty tablecloth that is only used for space clearing/cleansing your home and place the following on the table (see example at the end of chapter 3:

- bell
- harmony balls
- crystal
- a dish of sea salt
- a flower arrangement
- incense stick and holder
- atomiser containing your bush flower essences

- white sage
- matches

Then in each room (don't include bathrooms or toilets) place:
- small flower arrangement
- Incense and holder
- small tealight/holder (if not in your flower arrangement)

<u>Put sea salt across the outside of main doors</u> - Sea salt cleanses and heals. This can be removed after 24 hours.

<u>Write your wish list</u> - Write a wish list of everything you want to happen in the future and all your goals and aspirations. We are not just talking small stuff, dream big. "Where intention goes, energy flows".

How to write your wish list:

- Always start your wish with 'Thank You'
- Write in the present tense (like you already have it – be specific)

- Finish with "may this or something better now manifest itself for the greater good of all concerned".
- It can be as **long** or as **short** as you wish and can be either handwritten or typed.

An example of what you might write on your wish list:

Thank you for a happy and healthy home

Thank you for my income being plentiful

Thank you for my new black Range Rover Sports car

Thank you for getting grade 7 and above in all my GCSE exams

May this or something better now manifest itself for the greater good off all concerned

Fill your harmony balls with your intentions - Sit with your harmony balls in your right hand (the side of intuition) read your list and fill the balls with all the things you would like to happen, remember to include peace, love and harmony.

Date and keep your list and place it in the helpful friends or future area of your home (see chapter 7).

"The more energy and care you put into your cleanse, the greater results"

Chapter 6

'The Cleansing'

First, you need to Purify and Cleanse your space, as follows:

<u>Drink plenty of water:</u> Try to drink as you work and remember to breathe (no alcohol 24 hours before).

<u>Think about what you want to achieve</u>: For example, I would just say to myself *"I am here to cleanse my house. I am here to clear any negative energy from this house and replace it with positive energy for the good of all who live and visit here.*

<u>Circle your building/space and light candles and incense:</u> Walk clockwise and stay focused. Where you have placed all your flowers etc in each room, light the candle and then light the incense from the candle – always thinking about clearing negative energy. Arrive back to the starting position.

<u>Use the sage to clear away any negative energy:</u> American white sage is best. Take a fireproof dish and hold your sage stick above it (if you are using loose sage then place this in your fireproof bowl). Then, use the candle or lighter flame to light the end of the sage stick slowly. Any excess ash or embers will fall into the fireproof dish below. Slowly, a flame will ignite. Blow on the fire lightly to extinguish the flame. The sage stick will release healing smoke, similar to an incense stick. Whilst doing this keep repeating to yourself "clear negative energy".

Walk around your home clockwise wafting the sage on to the walls. Wherever you look the sage will go , even if you cannot reach. You may have to relight the sage a couple of times depending on how big the space is. Get in all the nooks and crannies, corners and crevices too. The goal is to keep the smoke moving lightly and efficiently through your home.

After you've smudged your entire home, your sage stick may still be smoking. Grab your ashtray or pot of sand. Gently press the stick into the pot until the smoke ceases. If its loose sage, I just run it under the tap and throw it away.

Cleanse my Home

Purify and harmonise Doing the same walk around your home with your bell and 'pull' the sound around the walls – you don't want to full on ring the bell constantly, just a little ring then move with the sound and keep repeating. You should be thinking about purifying and harmonising the space whilst you are ringing the bell. When you finish at the front door make the figure 8 (the sign of eternity) with your bell.

Next you want to put what you want (all you positive thoughts, goals and aspirations) into your home/space:

Harmony Balls Do the same walk again around your home with your harmony balls. The harmony balls have all your intentions in them. Visualise stardust coming from them as you shake them (all your words are in the star dust). You are filling your space with good intentions.

Spray Atomiser With your bush flower essences, again walk around your house clockwise whilst spraying your atomiser.

Lastly, preserve your work and space

Visualise a seal around your home to preserve your work - white light, gold mesh and a magenta cloak or pink pyramid.

*****

Cleanse my Home

Optional extra

Now, I do the following which involves angels and prayers (which isn't everyone's cup of tea!). As long as you have sealed your work, you can omit the following if it's not your thing:

Ask for four angels to stay (one in each corner of the house) to love, guide, support and protect everyone living in the house until you next space clear.

Say a prayer
I tend to use Psalm 121 because I like the wording and it protects people coming in and out of their house. You can also use The Prayer of consecration; I always put my right hand on the door when saying this prayer:

Psalm 121

[1] I will lift up my eyes to the hills—
From whence comes my help?
[2] My help *comes* from the LORD,
Who made heaven and earth.
[3] He will not allow your foot to be moved;
He who keeps you will not slumber.

⁴ Behold, He who keeps Israel
Shall neither slumber nor sleep.
⁵ The LORD *is* your keeper;
The LORD *is* your shade at your right hand.
⁶ The sun shall not strike you by day,
Nor the moon by night.
⁷ The LORD shall preserve you from all evil;
He shall preserve your soul.
⁸ The LORD shall preserve you're going out and you're coming in
From this time forth, and even forevermore.

After saying the above prayer, I finish by saying the following:

"I ask the highest and purest energies of divine love and light to lift and transform: Any historical negative energy attached to this space"

"I ask the highest and purest energies of divine love and light to lift and transform: Any geopathic stress attached to this space"

"I ask the highest and purest energies of divine love and light to lift and transform: Any other negative energy attached to this space"

"I ask the highest and purest energies of divine

love and light to lift and transform: Any lost souls attached to this space - and we would thank the angels for taking them to the light with love, compassion and forgiveness"

*****

To summarise the cleansing ceremony:

- Set a table with your bell, harmony balls, salt, flower arrangement, crystal, incense and spray.
- Put offerings in each room
- Write your list and fill your harmony balls
- Put your protection in place
- Announce your intentions
- Remove jewellery
- Sprinkle salt across doorways
- Light candles and incense
- Smudge sage
- Purify and harmonise using bell
- Harmony balls
- Spray atomiser
- Seal your work
- Say a prayer

Chapter 7

Australian Bush Flower Essences

Several cultures have used Flower Essences - the Egyptians, European and Aboriginal have all used them for centuries. In the fifteenth century Paracelsus, the mystic and healer, recorded the use of Flower Essences for emotional imbalances. In the 1930's Dr Bach (a pathologist, immunologist and bacteriologist) rejected his medical practice to dedicate his life to developing a simple and inexpensive form of medicine that ordinary people could use to heal themselves.

Dr Bach came to the conclusion, like Hippocrates and Paracelsus, that good health came from emotional, mental and spiritual harmony. To treat the emotional and psychological symptoms affecting people, their disease was cured. Dr Bach believed the Flower Essences cleared blocks that stop an individual getting in touch with their higher self (ie intuition).

Australia is relatively free of pollution and does not have the nuclear pollution or acid rain that other continents have. It has less pollution (i.e. pesticides and fertilisers) in the water tables. The Australian Bush Flower Essences help clear negative beliefs, attitudes and blockages that people have. Here are a few examples of essences that can be used in space clearing:

Angelsword
This essence allows access and retrieval of previously developed gifts from past lives. Angelsword protects from outside influences and entities so one can receive clear information from one's higher self without interference. Whilst fringed violet works to repair damage to the aura, Angelsword releases any energies that entered while the aura was open.

Fringed Violet
For treating damage to the aura where there has been shock, grief or distress (ie from abuse and assault). This remedy maintains psychic protection, especially for those working in psychic areas.

Lichen
A violent or sudden death can increase the likelihood of a spirit staying earthbound. People who commit suicide usually, as a karmic penalty, have to spend a certain amount of time on the astral before going to the light. In this situation the spraying of lichen from an atomiser will assist the soul to deal with existing on the astral and can speed up the time required before they go through the light.

Boab
This is one of the most powerful of all the bush essences and has brought about profound change. Boab clears negative, emotional and mental family patterns that are passed on from generation to generation. Boab can access and clear those core patterns and all the related ensuing beliefs. This essence is very beneficial in helping those who have had experience of abuse or prejudice from others. Also Boab will help clear the

negative lines of karma between people. When used in a spray it can be very effective in clearing negative energies, especially when combined with Fringed Violet, Angelsword and Lichen. Boab can help break the chains that have been around humans conscience for thousands of years.

Bottlebrush
This essence helps people move through major life changes and the overwhelming oppression that often goes with those changes, especially retirement, menopause, adolescence, death etc. It 'brushes' out the past and allows the person to move on.

Dagger Hakea

For people who feel resentment and bitterness, and hold grudges against those with whom they have been very close (i.e. family members and past lovers). This resentment is often not openly displayed. The plant gets its name from the needle-like barb that grows on its leaves.

Cleanse my Home

Flannel Flower

The petals in this flower resemble the sensuous texture of flannel. It almost begs to be touched and felt. This essence is for people who are uncomfortable with physical contact and touching. They often have difficulty in maintaining their personal boundaries. It is primarily for males, allowing for a gentleness, softness and sensitivity in touching. It helps one trust and express, especially verbal, their inner feelings. It brings enjoyment to physical expression for both males and females.

Red Lily

Red Lily is the same flower as the Sacred Lotus in the Buddhist tradition. It is for spirituality and connection to God in a grounded and centered way, allowing a person to have a wholeness to their spirituality by also realising the need to develop and maintain a balanced physical and emotional life.

To mix:

Use no more than four essences. In a 30ml atomiser, 7 drops of each essence, 2 drops of lavender oil and one teaspoon of Vodka. Top up with SPRING water.

I personally always use Angelsword, Fringed Violet and Boab and then depending on circumstances decide on which of the other essence fits requirements.

As already mentioned in Chapter 3, you can also buy ready-made space clearing spray. There is a very good one available from Australian Bush Flower which contains angelsword, boab, fringed violet, lichen and red lily.

Chapter 8
Feng Shui

Introduction to Feng Shui

This isn't a book on Feng Shui, I just wanted to cover the basics that I think may help and be of interest. However, if you would like more information about Feng Shui please see my reading recommendations at the end of this book.

Feng Shui is the Chinese art of placement dating back 4000 years. Literally translated, the words Feng Shui (pronounced fung schway) mean 'wind and water'. In practice, Feng Shui is concerned with living in harmony with your environment for health, wealth and happiness.

In all our lives, what we aim to achieve is balance, a sense of harmony both within ourselves and our surroundings. By thinking about the energies within you and around you and making constructive changes to create beneficial effects in the movement of those energies, you will make changes in your life by actively affecting your own good fortune.

Top 10 Feng Shui Tips *(taken from 'Feng Shui House Book' by Gina Lazenby)*

1. Make room for the new. Less is definitely more. Physical objects take up space in your life and can block the way for intangible things like opportunities or new connections with people to come your way. A big clear out will make space for your future. <u>Get rid of clutter.</u>

2. Make sure opportunity can knock on your door. If you want lady luck to find you then make sure she can see your front door and that there is a knocker or a working doorbell so that you can hear when she comes. Your front entrance needs to be clearly identifiable, easy to see and it should reflect how you want to be seen in the world, so don't let it get too scruffy. First impressions are very important.

3. Allow energy to flow freely. Invisible energy (or Ch'i) flows around your home bringing health and good fortune with it. Don't inhibit its flow by having too much stuff or furniture, or by having awkwardly placed pieces, that block it or inhibit its flow. Your home is a mirror for your life - if it feels good and clear so will you.

Cleanse my Home

4. Hold vital energy in. Energy needs to be able to meander slowly around your home and nourish you so avoid situations that allow it to move too quickly and leave before it has had a chance to do this. Back doors aligned directly with front doors with a long corridor in between summon the energy straight out of the back of the home in a great 'whoosh'. Money will come into the household but will go out just as fast. Put pots of plants down the corridor to break the straightness and hang a windchime to moderate the fast flow.

5. Make sure everything works. If you home works so will your life. Keep on top of the maintenance and fix things as they get broken. Replace the light bulbs and hang shades over bare bulbs. Every job left half done reflects some aspect of your life that is incomplete and needs attention.

6. Check out your home for negative energies. Understand that the invisible world of vibration is as important, if not more, than the physical world that you see. The earth has an electro-magnetic field which keeps us healthy. When natural radiation from the earth gets

distorted it becomes unhealthy for us. That is when we get geopathic stress running through a building and this is particularly harmful when lines of it cross our beds (see chapter 10).

7. Have you already got what you have been asking for? Our homes are mirrors for our lives and they can often reflect who and where we have been , not who we would like to be in the future or where we would love to go. Our choice of art and ornaments is always a message from our subconscious, so look around and see what you may have unwittingly been projecting into your space and asking for. An abundance of pictures of single women is definitely a silent request for a solitary life. Look around for symbols that repeat themselves and for recurring themes. If they represent what you have now got and that is what you want - brilliant - if not, change the art to reflect what you want for your future.

8. Create a quiet sanctuary for your bedroom. There is a lot of stress, conflict and uncertainty going on out there in the big wide world, so you need to retreat into the safe haven of your home. One of the places from which you get the most nourishment and support in your

bedroom, so it is important that this room be totally focused on restful sleep and not multiactivity centre. If you do have to work from your bedroom, hide all traces of it at night and cover mirrors as they expand energy.

9. Make the kitchen a centre of calm. This room is the most important in the home and is often the hub of family life. Make sure that it is not too busy and there is a quiet contained area where you can prepare food since this quality of calmness will go into the food we eat. Conversely, the more your kitchen resembles a fast-food takeaway, the brisker and less stable the energy that will be transferred into your meals - and into your life. You don't want to take stress in through your food too!

10. Love your home and it will love you. Think of your home as a living entity, care for it and it will care for you, making you feel supported and nourished and more able to deal with the things around you in the world which you cannot change. You can change your home and by doing so, you can transform your life.

Chapter 9

The Bagua

One of the first points of confusion in using feng shui is the bagua, or the feng shui energy map. The bagua is the main tool that you use in mapping your home to find out specific feng shui areas, or energetic spots that reveal how your environment is connected to various areas of your life.

Here is the basic bagua, I have kept it simple and only shown the areas of the bagua (instructions on how to use are at the end of this chapter):

Wealth	Success, recognition	Relationships
Family	Health	Future
Knowledge	Career	Helpful friends/travel

When you have defined the bagua of your home (or office), you then know the location of your love area, career area, wealth area, etc. The bagua is the tool that allows you to see this connection, as well as apply specific feng shui tips to balance and strengthen the areas that need help.

There are two types of method of using your bagua – The Front Door method or the Compass method. I've always used the front door method, it is easier to use and I have better results using the front door method.

It is always advisable to clear clutter in your home before you start to work on an area. Sometimes clearing clutter is all that is needed.

The areas of the bagua within your home are listed below. Each area within the bagua relates to an area in your home. Pictures and ornaments can be symbolic and reflect what is happening in your life in any given area.

1. Career

This area is known as career, it can represent new beginnings and opportunities, as well as how you are earning money. Use an enhancement in this area to improve your career or to change your direction. It will also help things flow (as in water). A plant in a black or blue pot, or a picture of a water scene (not stormy seas), or fountains are good - upward energy. A ship or boat coming towards you, not going away from you, would also be good. To move from one career to another, try a picture of a bridge.

2. Relationships

Relationships with your partner, work colleagues and family are connected with this area. An enhancement here would help a marriage or someone looking for a partner, or a better working relationship. Flowers or plants (pink and yellow), or a framed photo of a happy couple would activate the energy here.

3. Family

This area relates to parents and ancestors, your past and teachers. Placing a wooden framed photograph of your parents and grandparents here would be excellent. The colour is green - so a plant could be placed here. Any ornaments or symbols should always be placed as a pair in this area.

4. Wealth

This is the area of wealth and good luck. Place a money plant here or a bunch of red flowers. Fish are symbolic of wealth, so a picture, ornament or fish money box could be placed here.

5. Health

This area is the centre of the home. Good health is the centre of happiness. Always ensure that this area is free from clutter - especially if anyone has health problems. This can also be applied to the centre of each room.

6. Helpful friends, travel, cash flow

We all need helpful friends! A peace lily in a white pot or a white candle in a metal holder would enhance this area. If you would like to travel to more places, a globe or a map of the world would work here. A picture of angles here might mean 'friends in higher places'.

7. Creativity, children, future

This area covers your children and anything you create. Place plants, white flowers and pictures of your children here. This is also your future so have a picture or painting here of something you wish to bring into your life.

8. Knowledge

Place books in this area for learning. This area also relates to your religious beliefs and your intuition. A picture connected to love and harmony or yellow flowers, would enhance this area.

9.   Fame, status

This area relates to fame, recognition and status. It also relates to spiritual enlightenment. If you need more clarity in your life place red flowers, a red object of burn a candle in this area.

*****

How to use a Bagua:

Your first step is to apply the bagua to your home's floor plan (the main floor).

1. Use an accurately scaled floor plan of your home (or room), I find this easier to do on graph paper.
2. Rotate the plan so the wall with the front door is at the bottom.
3. Overlay a three-by-three grid, with the bottom of the grid aligned with the wall with the front door.
4. Make sure the grid is equally spaced.
5. Locate all the areas to match up with the bagua. Note: Knowledge, Career, and Helpful Friends should always be aligned with the bottom (wall with the front door).
6. Examples are at the end of the chapter!

*****

One very common feng shui issue is having a "missing" area in a property. For example, a property may be L-shaped and therefore have its wealth area "missing." If you have a difficult or complicated floor plan, try to apply the bagua just over your bedroom. Bedrooms are typically a regular shape that makes it easier. In addition, the most effective place to work on your feng shui is your bedroom, because it's the space that's closest to you.

However, this isn't a book on feng shui or the bagua, therefore if you feel you need further information, there is a recommended further reading list at the end of the book.

*****

Here is the bagua again and I will now show you how I have used in on a floor plan:

Wealth	Success, recognition	Relationships
Family	Health	Future
Knowledge	Career	Helpful friends/travel

PLACE THE BOTTOM OF THE BAGUA AT FRONT ENTRANCE

*****

This is an example of my downstairs floor plan, drawn on graph paper. As you can see my front door is to the bottom left, which falls in the

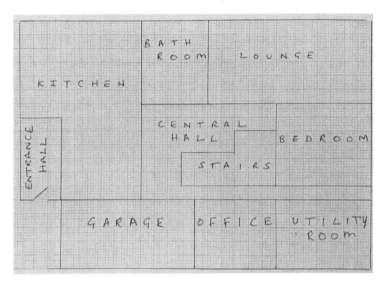

knowledge area of the bagua (your front door will always fall either in knowledge, career or the travel area).

This is an example of my downstairs floor plan, with the three-by-three grid drawn over the top of the plan. I have then written in the relevant areas of the plan:

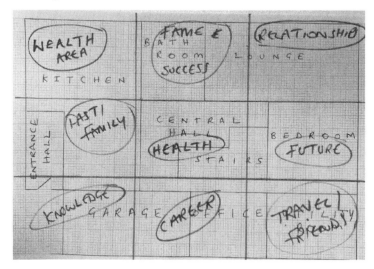

I have done another quick example of laying the bagua over a bedroom (as opposed to a whole house). The room is long and narrow so the bagua reflects this shape, note the door into the bedroom is in the career area this time:

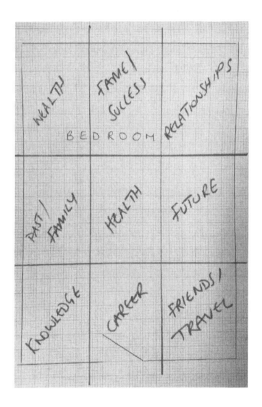

As I write this book, my daughters are currently studying for their GCSEs. I have therefore enhanced the knowledge area of the house (which if you look on the map is part in the kitchen and in the garage) by placing a yellow plant in my kitchen. I will also enhance that area in both of their bedrooms.

Lastly, some people are naturally in tune with the energy around them. So if everything in your life is running smoothly and well, my only advice would be *don't try and fix something that isn't broke*!

Chapter 10

Geopathic Stress

<u>What is geopathic stress?</u>
The impacts that can occur to individuals (and animals) who spend time living, working, or sleeping above dangerous subsurface magnetic fields are referred to as "geopathic stress." It is claimed that once the subsurface earth energies have been altered, our bodies' energy fields may no longer be compatible with the sun's natural beams. Practically speaking, people are likely to experience effects if their home, workplace, etc. is situated even slightly above these dangerous rays. This is frequently known as "sick building syndrome."

Distortion occurs as certain fields of energy rise to the earth's surface through subsurface fissures, fractures, cavities, mine workings, underground running water, and specific minerals.

Railway cuttings, motorways or building foundations, tunnels and embankments, mines and quarries - all will cause trauma to the earth.

A sign that you may have geopathic stress in your house are things going wrong, illness or arguments. I tend to be able to feel when geopathic stress has returned (as the earth has movement in it all the time). It is always good to check for geopathic stress when you are clearing a house of negative energy, as both go hand in hand. You can do this by dowsing either with dowsing rods or a pendulum. This is called geomancy.

There are a couple of ways to clear geopathic stress from your house, from earth acupuncture and crystals. You can also buy devices that clear it for you, however these tend to be very expensive.

<u>What is earth acupuncture?</u>
Earth acupuncture is a technique used by geomancers to remedy geopathic stress. Metal or copper stakes are gently placed into carefully dowsed earth acupuncture points and remain only as long as is needed to harmonise the line.

Like the human body, the earth is crisscrossed with meridians (lines of energy), the flow of which can become blocked or stagnated. This can occur naturally or can be caused by human activity, such as building work (e.g. laying foundations of a home), quarrying, road and rail construction, tunnels, drains, landfill sites, or traumatic events. These blocks or stagnations are called geopathic stress, and they can have a detrimental impact on the health of anyone who spends a lot of time in their vicinity. Using earth acupuncture, the geomancer can treat and harmonise such imbalances.

A good practitioner can also use crystals to harmonise lines of geopathic stress. It is not always possible to put stakes into the ground (eg, if someone lives in a flat/apartment) therefore crystals are a very good option for treating lines of geopathic stress.

*****

Crystals

I personally like to use either selenite or tourmaline, but there are a number of different crystals you can use:

Tourmaline
Tourmaline is one of the most popular stones for geopathic stress, and is available in colours like black, yellow, red, pink, blue-green, etc. Black tourmaline is also known as 'Schorl', and is a purifying crystal that protects the person against negative energies, radiations, and electromagnetic smog. It can be placed in the corners of your home, or anywhere in the house.

Selenite
A fragile crystal, *selenite* has the ability to block stale energy, extinguish negativity, and magnify positive energy forces. It is believed to have a calming effect, and helps bring about a sense of peace in the house. It can be placed anywhere, though placing it on the area of geopathic stress zones can bring about the maximum positive effect.

Shungite

Shungite is a brilliant crystal which has astonishing healing properties that are believed to protect the person against electromagnetic radiations from Wi-Fi routers, cell phones, laptops, etc. This crystal also helps ground a person, transfers the excess charge to the Earth, and neutralizes geopathic stress.

This is a crystal that is believed to radiate peace and calm. It brings out the positivity and optimism in a person. In fact, it is one of the few stones that is believed to exude love and affection.

This stone can be placed near any electronic device like cell phones, radio, television, laptops, etc. It is a rather popular stone, and provides incredible results with regard to cleansing geopathic stress lines. It helps neutralize electric currents and protects the house from any harm. In fact, it is believed to transform negative energy from digital devices to positive energy.

Kunzite

Kunzite is a highly protective crystal and helps deflect negative radiation. It is a good idea to place it close to microwave ovens; the stone is likely to clear the area of electromagnetic smog and pollution. It is available in very attractive colours like yellow, lilac, pink, etc., and is readily available in almost all parts of the world.

Lepidolite

Lepidolite is generally available in shades of lilac or pink. It has special properties to clear up electromagnetic smog, especially when placed close to electronic devices like computers.

This stone is popularly used to make attractive jewellery. However, it is a highly protective stone as well. It grounds negative energy, neutralizes harmful radiation, and helps purify the house from geopathic stress.

Agate

Agate is supposed to be a highly powerful stone. This crystal balances the positive and negative energies in the environment and helps maintain equilibrium. It has innumerable benefits – it helps soothe the senses, maintain calm, develop self-confidence, stimulate memory, enhance concentration, etc.

Again, this isn't a book on geopathic stress, this chapter is to make you aware of it and the problems it can bring. If you think you have geopathic stress you need to call a trained geomancer to come in a clear it for you. If in any doubt you can contact me for further information or help (my details are at the end of the book).

Chapter 11
BONUS CHAPTER
'THE WISH BOMB'

Use this ceremony in space clearing to help solve a specific problem or argument or intense emotions. Use if someone has been ill. Use when something extra is needed to shift things.

<u>What you need</u>:

Large saucepan with lid or a deep pyrex bowl

A metal stand or grid

2 small glasses

80g rock salt

100ml alcohol (has to be 40%)

Long matches

<u>Directions</u>:

- Switch off the telephone/mobile;

- Invite partner or whoever is helping/needs help to sit opposite (or work alone);
- Place protection around you and them;
- Call in guides and angels to help;
- Take the glass of alcohol and thank the water element. Pour slowly with intent into the saucepan;
- Take the glass of salt and thank mother earth, place carefully into the saucepan;
- Take a match and thank the fire element, strike with intention and light the salt;
- Watch the fire and stay focused;
- Place intention into the fire and watch for visions or listen for words.

You can also write on a sheet of paper what you would like to happen or bring into your life. This helps you focus your intentions. You could keep a second copy in your helpful friends area (see chapter 9 for further details).

Hold the paper in your hand and charge it with positive energy, then as the fire is burning low, place into the pan.

Watch it burn knowing that as it converts to ashes and smoke, your wishes are rising to the unseen realms so the creator can help move dreams into

Cleanse my Home

reality. You can scatter the contents of the pan around the outside of the home.

SUMMARY

I really do hope you have enjoyed the book and have gained an insight into the art of cleansing your home.

It has been a very cathartic process writing this book, space clearing is something I have been doing for a long time and I have always had very positive results from the process. I hope that my knowledge and passion has come across in the book.

To get the most from the book, I suggest you read it once to get a basic understanding then re-read, make notes and then make a start!

I have also included a space at the back of the book for your to make notes and to write a wish list.

*****

I am happy to answer any questions on email and I can be contacted on:

CLEANSEMYHOUSE@GMAIL.COM

If you want to cleanse your house but you feel uncomfortable doing it yourself, or you think you may have geopathic stress, please go to my website www.cleansemyhome.com for further information on consultations.

BIBLIOGRAPHY AND FURTHER READING

Feng Shui Made Easy
William Spear

Feng Shui House Book
Gina Lazenby

Psychic Protection
William Bloom

Are You Sleeping in a Safe Place
Rolf Gordon

Geopathic Stress
Jane Thurnell-Read

Clearing your Clutter
Karen Kingston

Australian Bush Flower Remedies
Ian White

MY WISH LIST

Thank you for:

-
-
-
-
-
-
-
-
-
-

May this or something better manifest itself now for the great good of all concerned.

Cleanse my Home

NOTES

Printed in Great Britain
by Amazon